Heavenly Life

Ramsey Nasr

Heavenly Life
Selected Poems

Translated from the Dutch
by David Colmer

Banipal Books

First published in the UK by Banipal Books, London 2010

The poems in this collection were translated by
David Colmer from works selected by Ramsey Nasr from the
poet's poetry collections *27 gedichten & Geen lied (Thomas
Rap, 2000)*, *onhandig bloesemend* and *onze-lieve-vrouwe-zeppelin*
(De Bezige Bij, 2004 and 2006 respectively)
and other publications

A CIP record for this book is available in the British Library
ISBN 978-0-9549666-9-0

Banipal Books gratefully acknowledges the support of the Dutch
Foundation for Literature which has made this publication possible

Banipal Books
1 Gough Square, LONDON EC4A 3DE, UK
www.banipal.co.uk

Set in Bembo
Printed and bound in the UK

Poet Laureate of the Netherlands

Ramsey Nasr

Selected Poems

Heavenly Life

Translated from the Dutch
by David Colmer

Banipal Books

CONTENTS

From *27 gedichten & Geen lied*
(27 Poems & No Song)

From *onhandig bloesemend*
(awkwardly flowering)

From the cycle *dichter liefde* (poet love)

winter sonata (without viola and piano)

From *onze-lieve-vrouwe-zeppelin* (our lady zeppelin)

Becoming Poet Laureate

Poems written in the function of Poet Laureate of the Netherlands

Foreword

Ramsey Nasr has written and performed prize-winning monologues, played Romeo in Romeo and Juliet, directed opera singers in Mozart's *Die Entführung aus dem Serail* alongside a classical Arabic singer, writes essays for Dutch and Flemish media on art and politics, and in 2006 was awarded the prize of Journalist for Peace. But poems are the centre of his work and and like all the best poems his are rooted in both music and history. He has embedded a series on Antwerp, for instance, in historical commentary and photographs of the city.

In every form, Nasr's work speaks of historical context and a historical imagination which is inextricable from his Palestinian descent. His father came from Salfit in the West Bank. In 1978 soldiers entered his father's land and oversaw the building of what is now one of Israel's largest settlements. That is why the generous universality of his poems is so remarkable. On becoming Poet Laureate of the Netherlands last year, he wrote a poem inspired by Vermeer's 'Woman Holding a Balance' and balance is key to his work. His meditation on Jewish music played under the Third Reich stands for us all. Art – as he quotes – 'is a sun/ that must shine for all people'.

RUTH PADEL
London, September 2010

Every Tear's a Minus

The Poetry of Ramsey Nasr,
Poet Laureate of the Netherlands

At the start of his career Ramsey Nasr (Rotterdam, 1974) was invariably referred to as an 'actor/poet'. He himself had this to say on the subject: 'I began as an actor – that was what I did. When my first collection came out, I was suddenly dubbed an actor/poet. Initially I found it very odd. I didn't feel like a poet; I'd simply published some poems. In the past I always had a problem with the word "artist", which I felt was just a label they stuck on you. Now I know that I'm quite simply a poet and an artist. I have great respect for musicians and composers, but I don't play an instrument myself. I regard writing poetry as a kind of composing, in which, however, you are bound by meanings. But you can decide for yourself what a poem is going to mean.'

His first collection, *27 gedichten & Geen lied* (27 Poems & No Song, 2000), was well received and earned him a nomination for the début collection of the year. What was striking in the Dutch poetic climate was that Nasr wrote lyrically and frankly about love and sex. In contrast, many of his postmodern contemporaries avoided the word 'I' and the description of feelings, and instead, in poems remarkable for the absence of the first-person pronoun, focused on the problematic relationship with language and chaotic reality. Nasr's was obviously a different, unusual kind of voice: 'This is poetry that, come rain or come shine, strives for old-fashioned euphony and rhyme, and the most astonishing thing of all is the almost complete absence of understatement and scepticism. We hear the spirit of Roland Holst and Boutens [classic Dutch poets of the early twentieth century – VS], great, forgotten names,' wrote the critic Rob Schouten in a review.

However, it would be an over-simplification to argue that the poet simply turned the clock back a hundred years and abandoned himself to old-fashioned bombastic romanticism. Nasr avoided sentimentality through the use of unexpected turns of phrase: in one poem he plants a smacking kiss on a teacup instead of his lover, and elsewhere he compares physical love with the copulation of animals: *as if from lukewarm cheese the filth's sighed out.* In his work lovers sweated rather than swooned. His début contained mainly passionate poetry, which left absolutely no time for ironic distance. There is always something at stake, his attitude is always one of complete commitment, and he does not shirk the use of big words.

The epic poem *Geen lied* (No Song), the climax of the collection, presents an Orpheus-like figure who searches the underworld for his dead lover and returns to a world changed beyond recognition. In almost one thousand lines, using classical five-foot iambic metre, the poem sketches the dismantling of one man's youth. This treatment of an age-old theme did not prevent Nasr also being aware of what was happening in the world: the hopeless conflict between Israel and Palestine, a topic that was to recur constantly in his later work, is characterised in one line as 'a people that builds zebra crossings over wounds'.

Following his début Nasr published the playful novella *Kapitein Zeiksnor & De Twee Culturen* (Captain Sourpuss & the Two Cultures, 2001), two librettos in one volume, and directed a number of operas, by Mozart and others. He was in demand as a performer at home and abroad, and he read from his own work in, for example, Germany, Indonesia and the Netherlands Antilles.

During a series of appearances in Bethlehem, Ramallah, East Jerusalem and Amman, something strange happened: 'For the audiences there everything, absolutely everything was about Palestine and Israel. Every fragment centred on that single point, that one essential theme that lay like a blanket of doom over everyday life, every necessary action. (...) The poem *De geliefden* (The lovers), for instance, was basically about a humdrum fact: the break-up of a relationship. It concerned a woman who wants peace and – in order to spare the man and not to hurt him – cuts off all his senses one by one, until he stands in front of her like a lifeless figurehead and she can rest. Perhaps not very cheerful, but at any rate domestic and mundane. But for Arab audiences it was crystal clear what kind of poem they were listening to: it was about the throttling embrace of two peoples.' After the readings men in tears came to shake Nasr's hand, and it slowly dawned on him what linguistic confusion had produced. The realisation that a love poem could be interpreted as a statement of political commitment was the biggest surprise for the poet himself. The meaning of a poem depends on the person reading it and much less on the person who wrote it.

In 2004 his second collection, *onhandig bloesemend* (awkwardly flowering), appeared. What first caught the eye was the physical appearance of his poems: the poems were printed in a bold, sans-serif typeface without capitals, and fanned out over the page – hence the (almost) square format of the book. The collection consisted of two long poems. The first series, *dichter liefde* (poet love), centres on Fritz Wunderlich, the lyrical tenor who died at the peak of his fame and made his name with his performance of Schumann's *Dichterliebe*. Wunderlich has been transmogrified into the character of Frederik Wonderlik, and instead of making him a pining lover Nasr creates a character with both feet on the ground: *for love freddy wonderlick/ had already diluted imagery/ but now he knew for sure/ every tear's a minus.*

Romanticism is not – as a critic once wrongly observed – a movement to which Nasr subscribes, but the *subject* of his multi-layered and polyphonic poetry. Beauty is seen in perspective, as in the imagery from which the title is taken:

> *awkward when flowers keep sprouting from eyes*
> *rock-hard on stalks and then they open too*
> *in front of your nose of course why not*
> *you can't see a thing but hey they're your flowers*

Poetry has by definition something contorted, something awkward about it, but that is precisely the core of art, these lines seem to say. Nasr deliberately opts for words that have fallen into disuse, formulations that come perilously close to kitsch. For example, he writes: 'velvet petals', 'carmine', 'pearly teardrops', 'o full-pink dawn' and 'agony's urge'. The way in which these perfumed terms are used here is in fact progressive. The naivety of Frederik Wonderlik and his tragic love – in all its awkwardness and its excessive elegance – poignant because of the conviction and vulnerability with which it is professed. This is not safe, neatly tended poetry, but contemporary lyricism that dares to use an old-fashioned voice.

The high point of the collection is *wintersonate (zonder piano en altviool)* (winter sonata, without piano or viola), a three-part poem inspired by the life of Dmitri Shostakovich. Nasr based it on the viola sonata that the Russian composer wrote shortly before his death, and gives Shostakovich a speaking role from his deathbed – free-associating, at times jumping from one subject to another, and at others coming up with an observation (*I don't think much about my childhood any more)* or an aside (*I hate toscanini).* Just like Shostakovich's viola sonata, the cycle opens with a moderato movement, continues in allegretto and ends in an adagio. The composition is striking: where Nasr moves from moderato to allegretto, the tempo changes, and in the transition to the adagio the same thing happens. Every aspect of the theme and the style is a reflection of the original. As a bonus a short commentary on the death of the composer follows.

With its richness of colour and sound, *wintersonate* reflects the cultural climate of the former Soviet Union. Nasr cleverly identifies with the old, dying composer and gives a picture of a country ruled by Stalin. The second part makes for hilarious reading and especially listening, presenting us with a multi-coloured Soviet parade at which all kinds of absurd prizes are awarded, based upon prizes which Shostakovich actually won in his lifetime. 'communist privet', for example, wins the '2nd prize for the 2nd line of hedges at the bush competition on the 10th anniversary of the october revolution'. It is an intermezzo that shows how Nasr is able to integrate different voices from widely separated periods into his poetry.

At the end of 2004, a year after publication of *onhandig bloesemend* – awarded the Belgian Hugues C. Pernath Prize – Nasr was asked to become the city poet of Antwerp. This was a remarkable invitation since he was not in the strict sense a son of Antwerp, but a Dutchman, and on top of that one with a Palestinian father: 'In Antwerp I was the duty Dutchman (I wasn't identifiable as a Palestinian from the outside). (…) And then came that absurd request. Would I consider becoming city poet? I fell about laughing. I couldn't imagine there weren't any better candidates available. I also thought it was a crazy, almost perverse idea to call in a Dutch-Palestinian poet completely unknown to the people of Antwerp after Tom Lanoye (a celebrated Belgian writer and poet).

Nasr accepted the invitation because in ten years' time, as

he put it, he would have considered himself 'an insufferable coward' if he were to refuse. He immersed himself in the history of the city and realised in advance that it was pointless to write from the point of view of someone from Antwerp. Instead, he wrote with the eye of an outsider: you sometimes see things more acutely from a distance. Apart from that it wasn't his intention to write poems aimed solely at Antwerp readers, they were meant for any audience. For a year he wrote poems on occasions such as the opening of the municipal library and on typical symbols of Antwerp, such as the Zoo or an Antwerp-born celebrity.

Because of the response that Nasr met with from the outset – there was much positive feedback and his appearances were attended like pop concerts – it became clear to him that poetry, traditionally a genre with a limited scope, here had a chance to bridge the gap. Especially if you could express your commitment as city poet: for example, he wrote a poem about a young Muslim woman who received death threats because she wore a headscarf. She had finally taken it off out of fear but the threat remained.

He also wrote a poem based on interviews he had had with deprived people in Antwerp. The poem was put up on the front of the Antwerp Social Services building, an agency where such people often feel misunderstood. Yet many came to the unveiling and could not fight back tears. It was their coming-out, as they called it. The poems, published in various Belgian national newspapers, regularly sparked controversy. The collection of Antwerp city poems grew into a unified whole and was published in *onze-lieve-vrouwe-zeppelin* (our lady zeppelin, 2006), with an introduction and splendid historical photos of the city.

In the articles and columns that he has written for the Dutch and Flemish media, Nasr reveals himself as a man of many passions. These include a love of art – classical music, drama, poetry – as well as deep involvement in contemporary politics. One issue in particular is close to his heart: the Palestinian-Israeli conflict. A wide selection of these articles on art and politics appeared, together with his collection of Antwerp city poems, under the title *Van de vijand en de muzikant* (Of the enemy and the musician, 2006). In the collection he discussed a number of controversies surrounding his term as city poet, but also his admiration for Shostakovich (whose widow he does not dare speak to at a concert), plans to dismantle cultural policy, and journeys he had made.

The degree to which poetry and politics are intertwined was clear from a column written by Nasr on Israeli policy and the passive attitude of the Dutch government, which he published in the daily *NRC Handelsblad* when he was about to become city poet of Antwerp. He stressed the crucial importance of finally implementing the UN resolutions before it was too late. There were immediate reactions, for example in the *Belgisch Israëlitisch Weekblad*, and there were rumblings from the liberal conservative VLD political party. Nasr was accused of conducting a witch hunt. The Israeli ambassador was also 'deeply shocked', and there was a call for Nasr to be stripped of the post of city poet even before he had officially taken it up. He responded in a number of articles, including a story as simple as it was shattering, concerning his father: 'My father comes from a small town in the heart of the West Bank. It is near a fertile valley. Life was simple, but idyllic – so idyllic that one day in 1978 ten soldiers with two tents and one settler came marching up the neighbouring hill. They came to establish a new reality: Ariel. The development, built on our farmland, now has 45,000 inhabitants and they're going to build a wall around our town soon. To protect *them* from us.'

The question of Israel and the Occupied Territories is a constant thread through Nasr's work – obviously because of his father, but also because the subject is part of the clash between East and West that has flared up since 9/11. This left its mark on Dutch politics, with the murder of the controversial politician Pim Fortuyn just before the 2002 elections in which he would have made great gains, and the assassination of the director Theo van Gogh because of his collaboration on the film of Ayaan Hirsi Ali in which she expressed criticism of Islam. Besides these events, which can be regarded as national traumas, there was the rise of the even more populist Geert Wilders, who in a provocative way made the struggle against Islam his sole mission, and in the 2010 election gained one and a half million votes to head the third largest party in the Netherlands.

When Ramsey Nasr became Poet Laureate of the Netherlands at the beginning of 2009 – unlike in the UK, this was on the basis of an elected shortlist of candidates, each of whom is required to write a 'a proof of competence' – he announced that he particularly wished to reflect on Dutch identity. In an interview he said: 'The Netherlands is very preoccupied with reinventing itself, and I think that a poet can be of some help in that, not by giving the answers, but by raising questions. I myself find it interesting to reflect on the Dutch identity. Dutch people: who are they? As Dutch Laureate I have set myself the task of raising this question and writing a series of poems about it, in the hope that after four years a consistent whole might have been created.'

A year on, some very powerful and influential poems have appeared – including an attack on Prime Minister Jan-Peter Balkenende who, according to the report on the Netherlands' support for the invasion of Iraq, misinformed parliament and was economical with the truth, and dismissed that report immediately after its appearance. Nasr also protested against proposed severe cuts in the cultural sector, as announced by Geert Wilders, who in a notorious pronouncement labelled all art as a 'left-wing hobby'. In a country like the Netherlands we need a poet like Ramsey Nasr: he is someone who involves his country in poetry; and conversely, who shows poetry his country.

VICTOR SCHIFERLI
Amsterdam, September 2010

Translated from the Dutch by Paul Vincent

Heavenly Life
Selected Poems

Selections from
27 gedichten & Geen lied
(27 Poems & No Song)

Turn my Mother

Turn my mother into a garden to plant in the snow.
Creamy-white jasmine and roses grow white.
The fullest of sounds come deep from within
like fruit from a stone.

Turn my mother into chameleons both of them blind:
green he gambles stroking the chest
she's curling towards him the deepest of reds.
Something more beautiful might now arise.

Turn my mother into a cathedral of light in a box.
In the morning lift up the wooden lid and listen
to the many-voiced mass that begins
a celebration of loss.

Turn my mother into the same girl but iron.
Raise her this time with more powerful blows.
Console her or teach her some smart magic spells
because in this body she's dying.

Silly Juliet

Silly Juliet
what have you done
those eyes snuffed out
your throat squeezed shut
your gut run through
your fingers cut up
you've murdered your body
with silly silly thoughts
I am here
do you want me
do you want me to rise up to you
to push you up further
to pull you along
to give you my help
to learn to fly together
without letting go
toasting each other
two chambers one heart
I am coming my love
I put on my heavy wings
and rise
I rise
and on the way I'll count the stars for you
and planets too
with water sprinkling from my toes
I'll keep ten toes for you

and both my heels will shoot out light-blue gas
to bring me higher close to you
filth dripping from my eyes
and running down my cheeks
to fill up both my hands
they pour it out
far below
dead filth over dead earth
I am coming closer
I pick up speed
the skies around turn dark I call your name
I see the stars behind me fail
I see them slowly dim
while I squeeze flames from every hair
filaments that cover my body
my head is burning for you
my hands are ten pinions of radiant fire
I rise with my own power
no longer ascending
I am coming to you
my body melts away
my bones explode like hot swamp gas
I am radiant
feel my body swell and burst
veins arteries capillaries
nerves of light solidified as light for you
I've changed myself for you
I am searching now for you

I light you up from deep inside
I seek the edges of your hollow body
searching for your fingers
ten fingers for me
I am burning
I scorch bright inside you
do you feel me
I am coming to you my love
I am coming.

No Song

(excerpt from a long poem about Orpheus in the underworld trying to bring his beloved back from the dead)

He wants her to begin
and plants a tender kiss on her little toe.
At once it flares up as a small gas flame
a shimmering sapphire of deep-dark blue
a cold blue flame that lights a second toe.
The five blue-burning flames go tickling in
and with a second kiss from his stone lips
he wakes the other smallest toe as well.
It glows and grows until it's like a crown
of lazurite that's flaring up inside the dark
a fire of blue ignited by a whisper
now slowly pours into her thinnest nerves
from her toes up. Azure becomes more violet
creeping further through tiny merging vessels
that empty into ever larger vessels
becoming veins and turning purplish red.
They glow and other streams keep flowing in
joining together in an orange haze.
Extended strands start linking up together.
At first they shine like topaz, then sulphur.
Luminous yellow tubes search out a route
across the sand. Her legs once lay right here

where he now watches these two columns of light
approach each other quickly, faster and faster
shooting upward in ever broader rays
a pair of comets that burn each other up
twin stars that pulverise and crush each other
until a new and monstrous sun erupts.
From this hot sun is born a fluid pelvis
that opens, spreading wide, and then contracts
while it slowly, very slowly sets.
She lies here now, a mass of seething magma
beneath the piled, hot, half-molten rubble
that weighs her down. Miraculous debris.
Her upper body, so much afterbirth
the softest gem of all still swathed in pink
placental, sweet. Concentric rings of Saturn.
Everything is open now and while she sets
a hand slides in beneath her sizzling pelvis.
It moves along and slows between her legs.
It feels her lower back; the vertebrae
still burning hot and cartilaginous.
Trespassing under tender skin. My hand
around the naked discs. It gently tugs
to free them from the mass. Cuts out the pelvis.
It plucks the polished ribs out one by one
then very carefully removes the joints.
You lie here yieldingly, fragile no longer.
Two bright, translucent legs with veins of light
the hot white pelvis still unformed.

Beneath your flesh, your dormant upper body
which I'm now holding tightly in my arms.
My dancer's arm is pressing on your back.
A head, two arms that slowly circle in.
I'm here to move into your drum-tight skin
and when I step into your waiting pelvis
both my legs just melt away at once.
Two bodies come together at our waist.
There's nothing under us except ourselves.
Nothing between. We stand on paths of light
and burn inside. I'm screaming through your mouth.
Coloratura shooting left and right.
Our voices rise together. We step forth
and sing, encountering electricity –
a blinding, freezing flash – and then another.
A new location.

Selections from
onhandig bloesemend
(awkwardly flowering)

da capo

enter blackest of black
with your sand-blasted soul
and your scheduled tears
enter and roar like a lady

scream under a wooden curtain
again cadenza after cadenza
die in a body not your own
sing until it bleeds
                  I'm waiting

break the red hall open
I've got it clean and quiet
and beg you be my opera
da capo
              kiss this empty heart

the conspiracy

science laugh it off
but it's only natural
for crying out loud
it's never clicked between us
      the poet

      and you
measured man plus chemical woman
laboratory twins of progress
filling petri dishes together sure thing
explain that away
down white corridors I've heard otherwise
in immaculate coats exchanging
proteins between yourselves
nucleotide base pairs maybe
then whispering together
and why do you do it and who for
spit it out! what are you in god's name!
oh my god, up to

I've heard all this recently
from confident sources
but heed my words
and − read − lips − kiddo
or we too will cause disaster

with sheet lightning and titans' thunder
hold on to those richter scales
sincerely hold on to me
      hold me

     your poet

my aching head

my * aching * head * * * like * lumps
on * my * skull * being * hammered
flat * * * wait * * * today * I * will
look * up * the * width * of * everything
do * the * dishes * but * quietly
my * god * * * and * the * bottle
bank * * * remember * to * take * the
bottles * * * I * am * wrecked
just have * to * eat * tomorrow's
shit * and * then * * * what * does
contumely * mean * * * look * it
up * * * no * * * don't * look * it
up * * * go * to * bed * and * on
the * way * from * chair * to * bed
stand * still * and * cry * * * cry

under thor's hammer or
the hot drive to valhalla

nothing finer than the company of professors
try it sometime

drinking rilke with sprightly seniors
just stick in a straw and bloop
one by one they bubble up
the lost treasures of coblenz
the unsurpassed pavements of weimar
sind sie da wirklich noch nie gewesen
and that's not all

you can have long slabs of wolff
gulp down a little schiller too
gulp gulp with ears a-gurgle
suck them out with abandon
here comes
rückert rückert mörike mörike!
haben sie das wirklich noch nicht gelesen
that's really not all

yessss I am
stuffed to the top of my gills
but it only gets better
because then they go götz! götz!
those herren professoren doktoren pumping away

pouring out konwitschny son of konwitschny
the first georgian germanist
goethe's chromatics
not nearly as deranged as it seems
and then and only then (bloop)
when it really is coming
warm and runny out your nose
haben sie sie wirklich nicht gekannt
the complete life and times of frau tube-beckmann

one learns a lot in an hour or two
on a backseat
full in the sun
with the windows shut
elderly professors
left right left
around my monotone
my tired swelling
poor poor head

what am I the very first telephone
are you teutonic demons

I'd much rather have spent today
drinking thin simmering goat's yoghurt
two steaming bowls full

fox
(state of the union)

I am fox
tear out their throats
without cooking
eat chickens up

cross-eyed fucking chickens
stumblebum full
of eggs
so don't be chicken

be fox

be fox!

so
give up king craw
make no mistake
give in and up
for the last time

     EAT CHICKEN
     BE FOX

& god
bless
fox

final chorus

it isn't death that's freezing you
it isn't death that's stifling you
it's both of them and more
death's a leg up into darkness
the EXIT sign read back to front
death is kind infinite kindness
compared to this lifeless
falling falling from the curtain
fall

and the seats are empty and the stage is small
and the curtain has no seam no edge at all

the subhuman and his habitat

welcome to the land of milk and honey
where figalmondapricots grow
unmetaphorically on accommodating trees
eat of them and be my guest today
I'll pay your taxi to the first roadblock

my father waits behind the second roadblock
he'll make you his guest of honour too
with oil bread oregano sesame
stars lie motionless upon his roof
sleep there and give him nadir's love

the day to father is hard but essential
try to find a kid with a barrow
take donkeys or scramble on foot round the cliffs
follow the others keep telling yourself
now we are animals this is permissible

wheelchairs go bouncing through dust
back from the city where they cure the sick
diabetic with cancer in blazing sun
many are old many sick many are sweating animals
but that's the whole idea

in the day we are sweating climbing animals
because that's the whole idea
they beat and kick the animals to an end
that one day we will give milk and honey
one day manna will rain from human hands

if this seems insane to you habibi
just think that miles down the road
real girls and boys are sitting nervously
outside starbucks as an act of resistance
uproarious in fear of their lives

From the cycle of poems

dichter liefde

(poet love)

based on Schumann's/Heine's Dichterliebe

wondrous month

that was in the wondrous month
of excess and of blossomings
when my chest swirled up like poppies
ribs splaying like gaudy quills
may cut loose my stingy tongue
consuming similes like fire water

deeply shamed to my poldered soul
overcoated between the raindrop and the wind
insensitive to bushes branches thorns
I caught my death of light
                       and rubbed it in
transparent humiliating sparkle sneezing
came upon me a miracle there I went
less would be enough to shame the most
but this was my affliction utter love

salve and compresses by candlelight

awkward when flowers keep sprouting from eyes
rock-hard on stalks and then they open too
in front of your nose of course why not
you can't see a thing but hey they're your flowers

at night you sit there with salve and compresses by candlelight
trying to figure out
   how they grow there anyway dammit
      past lens and through iris
         a decent lachrymal papilla should
            manage that they clamp down on the point
               of crying I'm only guessing too
                  but maybe if I personally
                     if I tried to phone that canal of
                        schlemm pellet after pellet
until ruined and bloodshot
you fall asleep at last
with rustling reeds on your eyes

early next morning it's back to
cloying cherries left and right
stumbling down pink trails
bad for brains in the long run
and no good either is swearing
and hearing a choir of nighting-gulls

stay inside freddy wonderlick
sit on a chair at a table
and write that letter!

— to the love of my life —

if you are still willing to love
I will lovingly cut the flowers for you
I will put them in vases with fortifier
the two nighting-gulls glued
to your parents' windowsill
will look back grumbling as silently
we shrink into the healing night

the true lover

the rose the lily the dove the sun
monkey saturn the hydrogen bomb
love's bliss encompasses a lot of things
big and tangible they fit
easy in the mitts
of all-crumbling lovers

for them it's all:
    a. cuppa cha cuppa java
    b. ootchy-kootchy
    c. cuddly-snuggly honeybunny
    d. hi sweetie hi sugarplum

lovers trivialise the elements
a tad
stepping like armoured children
into their means of transport

sitting in their topsy-turvy choo-choo train
that's come to a standstill
for the second time this week
because of the silly chappie underneath

full of love he too
wanted to crush language
with his hands like them
but in his own way

he took steps
exploding himself from element
to vast delaying chaos
sudden thaw and frost in one

human bliss clings to stars and pollen
no miracle too big or small

for the blind with willpower
monkey is rose dove sun

the true lover admits no difference
between a lily and a hydrogen bomb

every tear a minus

the flowers used to know exactly
when and where young germans
with deeply wounded hearts
would appear in the bushes

pistils and all they homed in

by evening one heard
the sobbing crocuses and narcissi
even above the sound of the german
who'd come so far he was now trying
to dissuade some I'll-end-it-all bluebell

consolation was a way of life back then

the nighting-gull dropped by later too
no secrets in the woods those days
heavy hearts just pissed it off
it pealed those cheerful tones
sick bush turned into gleaming thicket
a constant flicking on and off
flashing blackberries and raspberries

the bush with the german
was now an enticing mini universe
come come cosmos

the stars stayed put
so far away so vast and all
but eight minutes later it came
full-blast from space
red-hot chunks of solace

and every day the same

nowadays you hawk your reject heart
door to door and no one's buying

germans are suddenly suspect
in this grey cankered city

for love freddy wonderlick
had already diluted imagery
but now he knew for sure
every tear's a minus

rare dawn

in the starting light of a summer's morn
I stand before a steaming greenhouse
flowers all whisp'ring murm'ling
and what are they talking about
and through which mouth
and why do I wander so muted
round said greenhouse in short
slow start to a morning in summer

the flowers chatter now behind panes
leaning back to watch me
it beggars belief with pity
"be not angry with our sister
you woeful paling man"

pinned between fleawort and gill-over-ground
I open my yet frozen mouth
behold my tongue

bulging out
resplendent woman
the object of my rare love

oh brilliant pink dawn
oh populous heart

bitter home

freddy wonderlick cries no more
no dreaming no arm pinching
when lying there cold as stone he saw
her become an unavoidable grave

day by day she grew irrefutable

calmly he hunted for remnants
lay awake beside her at night
found metaphors in bedside cabinets
pale cheeks bittersweet tears
lay sleeping next to smelly feet
he picked them up
not by jaws or scruff of neck but
bashed them still against the wall
hard to smithereens

new-fashioned now he doesn't cry
never belonged to anyone
awake for good in bitter home
freddy wonderlick lives on

credo

give me the head of a daft persistent into-the-ground runner
who rhymes heart with part cypress with red dead with hyacinth
scrapes his spilling confidence back together bending down

and won't stop organising stumble tours down trodden paths
tossing banana rhymes ahead he's imperturbable
half and off he calls them magic cobbles look

a bad joke told by a poet the way he rants and raves
leaping up sometimes for no reason snatching handfuls of air
but not always no not always and I prefer him far more

a thousand and one times more than scrimping king holland
with his battened modern voice behind his spiky table
wheelchair and handbrake no I'll manage or damage myself

also I loathe oracles of the order of the chocolate defecationists
pouring forth their broad brown nile certain of their infallible
                                                                delusion
confection-crapping a true vatican box full of chocolate liqueurs

                    I believe

in velure petals the ruined carmine of the sun's setting
the splendour-driven backward flight of the quetzal
his long emerald green tail awkwardly radiant for her

his ridiculous ostentation favouring life over death
and I believe in utter love it says what it says as if it's nothing

compared to liberian rebels gang rape is poetry too
I am attached to froth in all vanity I bear my night like a pouch

winter sonata
(without viola and piano)

based on the Viola Sonata, Op.147,
by Dmitri Shostakovich

in memoriam
Dmitri Dimitrievich Shostakovich (1906-1975)

I – moderato

death wants to be discussed
sine gloria straight
like a decahedron sandwich
like heaven in a basket small and stinking
a kick in the balls
to the bone if necessary
or a mouth full of tobacco something like that
but not abstract no
air to feed the poet the hermit no
tinselled baton for twirl-fisted men

death is not
kissing the iron bar that comes down massive
staring with bloody chops at the cheerful portrait
and waiting for new teeth
for the powerful
to line up again
attempting to kiss
instead of taking steps

do not ignore death either
doesn't help here he comes
very poorly disguised of course
this time a one-armed one-bunnied conjuror and look there's
the bar

he only has one trick
our oligophrenic practical joker
"look look come on look"
down comes the bar
he is alone again

no death is not much as food for thought
unless by way of pastime
some choice remains inside the falling house
mother wife daughter son
one mother upstairs in a chair
one wife standing next to you
two children asleep
ten seconds to think
(one child per arm)
three two one zero
which to save which to leave behind

who would
you really love?

and
if you could
in their stead

would you?

I stay in the burning house myself

blessed are the believers
they trust the bar that descends
cripples and crushes at random

but what can he do
the man who eats no air
rejects consolation like a pig's heart
and remembers everything with his hand
gut heart limbs
he has clamped down on his genitals
had perfect pitch excised
he eats the people's meat
like a good boy eats the plate the table the vodka
with bleeding chops but still I miss them

I miss I am ashamed
I miss my culled friends
like a beast

what to do

counterrevolutionary glands
secrete it like never before
enzymes produce it in buckets
loss

strange fluid in the cyst

the fault of my body
the fault of my teeth-spewing heart
but for the nicest leader of all time
I was ready to give it up

I will admit
that I have no power
over glands bowels and neurons
that I am struck dumb
like a clay statue with feet of wax
in the falling house

powerless I stand before you
pointlessly I came
to my own home
with tricks and imagery
a handful of feeble metaphors
or is there a cheerful cure
for cancer and infarcts of the heart?

someone has to tell me
someone stamps on my boiled sweets
one by one not yellow not red orange pink
blossoming black is what you are
inside and spreading further father
it does not look good
and not a doctor smart enough
for you to fix you up

so tell me

tell me
play piano left-handed
sing without breath limp
dignified but gallant

II – allegretto

then when one opens the sunroom doors
the sandalwood smell of dacha mixes
with outside air – the porch's offering
a view of imagination's culmination
the brave garden of the people's artists

in this garden approved and designed
by the most supreme leader of the proletarians
one finds what must almost inevitably be
the most glorious specimens from the
all-embracing ever-striving upward-aiming
floral realm if you please

take your time to stride around
the flowers a pageant passing by
notice those optimistic pistils
look there that simple striking shrub
what a solid plastic sea of flowers it is
and time to take the roll

present are

hydrangea
★   stalin prize 1st class

rhododendron
* 1st secretary of the flowers' union of the RSFSR

and *climbing rose* (see it sway and wave)
* people's flower of the bashkirian ASSR

also present with joyous rootstock
broom!
* vice-president of the plant division of the federation of
    associations for the promotion of the friendship of nations
* stalin prize 2nd class

behold *comrade gum*!
* honorary member of the serbian academy of artificial trees

behold *comrade snowdrop*!
* order of labour of the 2nd international seed-lobe festival
                                    in gottwaldov czechoslovakia
* stalin prize 1st class

behold *dear fuchsia*!
* people's chlorophyll of the RSFSR

and then I smell
chive!
* diploma and medallion from the peace committee of the
                                    soviet union

I smell
acanthus!
★ member of the committee for the accreditation of lenin
                                prizes flower and flora subdivisions

tulip!
★ lenin prize

comrade african violet!
★ doctor in the floral sciences of the USSR

communist larch!
★ glinka state prize 1st class
★ stalin prize 1st class

comrade edelweiss!
★ president of the austro-soviet friendship association and
        the federation of associations for the promotion of the
                                friendship of nations

communist privet!
★ 2nd prize for the 2nd hedge parade at the shrub
      competition marking the occasion of the 10th memorial
                        anniversary of the october revolution
★ stalin prize 1st class

comrade grass!
* member of the commission for decorative flowers, woods
                                             & legumes

and then yes then!
comrade potato!
* hero of socialist labour
* chairman of the tuber federation of the RSFSR
* member of the supreme soviet of the USSR for the
                                      district of gorki
* grosser stern der völkerfreundschaft in gold from the GDR
* stalin prize 1st class

the masses pass by and greet you!
from loudspeakers the song of the forest resounds
here scent of woodland path there essence of meadow and
                                      everywhere
everywhere musk!

concealed vaporisers in the beds spray at maximum
each now disseminating authentic scent in measured
triple doses festive!
stamens start to curl
oh friends of musk
all blooms will be moustaches!
brought to completion by the genius of the caucasus
gardener of gardeners!

the great day has dawned!
mushrooms wild and cultivated stamp! hum! the march of the
                                    fighters for peace
our motherland hears it!
our iron!
plastic motherland!

III – adagio

I agree fully with the statement in pravda
I am a worm

my childhood was not characterised by momentous events

(in the street soldiers broke up a crowd)
(a cossack cut down a boy)
(in those days streets were best avoided)

(in 1905 – I was not yet born
they stacked the murdered children on a sled
my parents often spoke of the events of 1905)

I rarely think of my childhood
I cannot recall a single event

I have little news
and even less good news
I broke my right leg
I broke my left leg
I suffer from headaches
I feel nauseous
my neck is swollen
my cheeks are bulging
my hand is ruined

I am now sure that I will never recover again
life does not really agree with me
in a manner of speaking
(I knew someone who had eight heart attacks
he is no longer with us)

fine
I am trying to remember
I shall try to speak the truth
why not after all

composition at the conservatory
is currently taught by the following
bogatyrev – shaporin – golubev – fere
probably someone else as well
in five or six days I will know more

I still remember who hurt me at the gymnasium and before

in my childhood I read a story that made a deep impression

one event I do remember:
an acquaintance of mine
an artiste performed in a cabaret called "crooked jimmy"

I was there when sollertinsky gave a shameless lady her
                                        comeuppance
(sollertinsky)

once I was at the philharmonic
they played stravinsky's "le rossignol"
as it were

in the cinemas "bed and sofa" was causing a stir

plenty of anecdotes about stanislavski did the rounds at the
                                                          time

(will you go away now
I cannot recall a single event
"the sun shines over our motherland")

my father loved gypsy romances
"the last chrysanthemums"
"the two bay laurels"
(he sang them)

(I admit I find it difficult in public)

I saw meyerhold's "queen of spades" in the maly theatre

I saw the revived "masquerade"

I wrote the music for "the bedbug"

I did not collaborate on mayakovsky's bad play "the bathhouse"

(I too find "hamlet" magnificent)

(I am trying to pull a hippo out of a swamp)

(...)

everyone knows that besides a musician borodin was also a
chemist...?

recently I went to get some lemonade in repino

(it is hard to summon up memories)

I adore mussorgsky
(his contemporaries called mussorgsky a dunce)

I have spoken to adults who were proud of not loving glinka

or not knowing him

I love glinka

I love the theatre

I love all kinds of social gatherings

my love of football knows no bounds

I like to be treated with respect

I do not like mayakovsky
(when I was introduced to mayakovsky he held out two fingers
in reply I held out one finger for him
he asked me if I liked fire brigade bands
I do not like mayakovsky)

I love chekhov deeply

I hate toscanini

I made a fabulous friend — sollertinsky
we spoke about death
he died and I was left behind
we were scared of death

in the old days people never listened when I spoke

(they claim that before going to concerts
glazunov stuffed his ears with cotton wool
to be alone with his thoughts
he had momentous thoughts)

I love glazunov

I love chamber music

I admit I find it difficult in public
our task is one of celebration
thank you for the conversation
"the motherland hears"
I believe that regarding myself I have been too
too much about myself

a few more words
I am scared of pain
I am scared of stepping over puddles
I think they are chasms

we haven't met
my name is shostakovich
if I might say so
I love glazunov

glazunov always got his alcohol at our place
they went about it like conspirators
(I still dream of glazunov's visits)

without erring glazunov picked out all the wrong notes
                                    wherever they were
he remembered when and how and how often each student
                                    had played wrong notes
especially telling from glazunov's mouth was the word
                                    "uncivilised"
glazunov was an aristocrat
glazunov was always busy
glazunov insisted that it was useful to write ballets
he lived his whole life with his mother
a voice as soft as a cockroach
and his enormous aquarium at home
glazunov enjoyed watching the fish and feeding them
I think he thought of an orchestra as a gleaming toy
he was thickset and overweight
until the revolution
he never stood up
finding it easier to stay seated
and keep playing
glazunov sat there at the piano in his fur coat
famous guest likewise in fur coat listening
smoke coming out of the mouths of felix weingartner
hermann abendroth
arthur schnabel and joseph szigeti
famous guests were astonished by glazunov
glazunov was astonished by them

he thought that if he died
something momentous would come to an end
that is why he did not die
becoming classic in his own lifetime

things like that should be repeated constantly
the time has now come
in which these things are necessary

I have a passionate love of music
I have dedicated myself totally to music
there are no pleasures in life besides music
everything about life is music
if they chop off my hands
I will persist with music
albeit pen in mouth

too often I think of meyerhold

I keep thinking I will break a leg

> sometimes I wanted to open my head completely like an arum lily
> and close it when convenient

everyone knew him
the circus clowns sang songs about meyerhold
combs were sold under the name meyerhold

"meyerhold lived in this building"
I stayed with vsevolod emilevich in novinsky boulevard

meyerhold loved to dress with elegance
raikh was a very beautiful woman
meyerhold was in love with her
raikh was enraptured by her own beauty

raikh was an energetic woman a kind of under-officer's widow
raikh was an outstanding haggler
marched to music by chopin
raikh sang glinka's romance while swinging her voluptuous
                              shoulders and giving knowing looks

they stabbed raikh
17 times and put out her eyes
raikh's screams went on and on
none of the neighbours came to help it could have been
                                                anything

"and in this building his wife was brutally murdered"

the name m. was no longer mentioned
and then the man disappeared

forgotten

sometimes I wished that like a lily
I could stand on stalin's wide table
pull myself up out of the vase
appraise him from a distance
my little gardener in his chair
my under-endowed flowerless plant
observing him
and ignoring him completely

we forgot zhilyayev too quickly

or nikolai vygodsky talented organist

pshibyshevsky head of the moscow conservatory he too was

                                            forgotten

son of the well-known writer pshibyshevsky

and dima gachev was forgotten
gachev was unlucky enough to speak french
he got five years
gachev was a strong man
a few days before the end they informed him that he had been

                                    given another ten years

that broke him

a specialist in the field of despair was zoshchenko
zoshchenko was considered a humorist
as punishment zoshchenko was underfed
his feet swelled up and not another line was published
he tried to stay alive
radiating joy

alexander germanovich preys died
he died young

forgotten

sollertinsky
arnshtam
balanchivadze
fleishman
vainberg
glikman
kustodiyev
nikolayev

in moscow there lived a famous person
by the name of tukhashevsky
tukhashevsky liked to be liked
with one outstretched arm he could lift a chair man and all by
                                                    a single leg
he was very handsome
we became friends

we walked a lot
tukhashevsky spoke quietly because he was afraid
I did it from despair
because many instruments were suspect (the trombone for
                                                    instance)
eighteen months later they shot him dead
I longed to disappear
(tukhashevsky)

sometimes I wanted to come up
like white lilac purple lilac
surrounding my friends
one by one in a loving shrub
suffocating them myself
smothering them here in my
two arms my red lilac

I would be so glad to see you again

(I cannot recall a single event)

I wanted to show that it is possible to kill people in more ways
                                            than just physically

"today a concert by the enemy of the people shostakovich"

death is close by
and many hands are being shaken

stalin was crazy about tarzan movies
he saw the whole series
stalin used to watch movies at night as well
he demanded that the entire politburo watch them with him
all of the country's leaders

he also loved going over menus
menus with caucasian wine

stalin had his own ideas about things

anyone could become a genius by order of the leader

comrade smirnov read me the libretto for a ballet
"the new machine"
the theme is extraordinarily relevant
once there was a machine
then it got broken
then it was fixed
and they bought a new one as well
then everyone danced around the new machine
climax

I have met musicians who assured me that stalin loved
                                                    beethoven
it was a time of many words oceans of words
you saw them devalue before your eyes

someone received a letter from america and was shot dead
and the allies kept sending letters
and each letter was a death sentence
each gift each souvenir the end

I got to look upon a saviour of mankind
small
fat and ruddy
his right arm thinner than his left
his face pockmarked
he did not resemble his portraits
he possessed no magical powers at all

I saw stalin and spoke with him
I was not scared

I am scared of pain

> *I wanted to be like a torch*
> *a trunk of burning mimosa*
> *so that I could lure him in the dark*
> *here comes the cossack moustache*
> *embrace him with cigarettes*
> *scorching away his kisses like moths*
> *and then glittering like mimosa*

you are not really the boss over your body

the human body is home to a constant array of unpleasant factors
I could not possibly say where my liver and bladder are located

I possess neither strength nor wisdom
I have little faith in eternity
death does not enthuse me
chekhov was not scared of death
gogol's fear of death brought his on
I do not sing death's praises
I am an observer by nature

I admit I find it difficult in public

the doctors talk about the sickness of my body
they probe and torment my body

but I am convinced it is my mind that is sick

I think everyone is looking at me
I think they are watching me
waiting for me to fall
or at least stumble

I feel attracted to people
when the lights go out and the piece begins I am almost happy
if I were invisible things would be better

everyone knows that with disease you must seek the cause
and then beat it out with a piece of wood

you know
they beat you but they never let you cry
our treatment is rough and cruel
others were less fortunate

in those days you had to take your guest to the bathroom to tell
                                                              a joke
in the bathroom you turned on the taps and with the noise of
                                                          the water
you could whisper your joke quietly laugh
hand over mouth

I am not exaggerating

american doctors said we are surprised by your courage
we leave americans cold

the high priests of medicine
have no answer to my question
which name to give this disease
I was sick I am sick
I learn to write with my left hand
gymnastics for the dying

I am dependent on doctors
I follow their orders meekly
I take all medications
but there is no diagnosis

I have tried to remember
a few times as best I could
I thought of all my friends
and saw only corpses

    I saw the bar that comes down

my friends
death is terrifying
with nothing behind it

I am behind you like a brick wall
darkness surrounds me

it is up to you

    ★   ★   ★

it was terrifying to see
how everything took place in the body
of the dead composer when his head
was finally stopped
laid aside
when the brain was disconnected

because now the sieve in the throat had collapsed
now the surging was over almost still
blood turning into misty vessels
with an appropriate final echo
now the heart seized the fateful moment
and sucked
sucked itself full in a fury
tugging with all its strength on both roots
sucking
feeding
cursing
and raging
like in a flower box

it seized upon rancour in the liver
scooped hatred up out of the stomach
stuffed itself with cancerous truffles
and gnawed at the skull
wolfing down contents
to grow

inflating between the ribs
terrifying to see
the way the heart didn't sink away
but hung there like a swollen shining
fleshy lantern

where were the doctors then
where was everyone
when like a heart
where were you
when it finally
like an open heart
when this swamp iris
this beauty of the night the morning glory
when finally as a firethorn it wanted
as a flower for you
when as a flower I
wanted to come to your arms as sweet chamomile
hold me tight
my honeysuckle
my shield fern
my bleeding heart
take me and hold me tight
I was belladonna turned to bitterwort
sundew and selfheal
like a sooty carnation
I was snakeroot
but different now

dwarf almond now
now
like a feverbush I wait
resplendent for you
like a gleaming medlar
with winter flame and bellflowers
hold me tight
my brightwhite evergold
I open now like sweet rocket
shoot up like st joseph's trumpet
and stork's beak
past jacob's ladder

up high
now I branch out
now

now mother of thousands

snowball bush

prince's feather now

now death

open and wide
terrifyingly wide

I feel no shame

awaiting you

there is no shame

and the music is bright
bright and clear

Selections from
onze-lieve-vrouwe-zeppelin
(our lady zeppelin)

The work immediately following was presented as
the sixth poem written by Ramsey Nasr in his
function of city poet of Antwerp. It deals with
poverty in Antwerp and was written after
conversations with some of the city's poor
inhabitants. It is now mounted on the wall of
Antwerp's social welfare service.

a minimum

read me then
and listen softly

I am the end
the dead-end man

for years my love
and I have been up

against this ceiling
of petty cash

rock bottom starts
where our skin ends

and there is no leeway
to wrap my arms around her

she's stuck between
I'm stuck beneath

and yes I have nothing
and sure I am nothing

but god almighty
I won't go under

till now I've fought
the years full
from the cradle
to the grave
I will struggle
against you
this ceiling
and all of the eyes
in your mouth

I will emerge
from my dole

to walk in the light of her day
with my underprivileged sun

and trumpet round

> *here we stand*
> *small and proud*
>
> *like a human*
> *on a square*

and I would not
swap with you

I would give
good money

to be myself
the way you are

The next two poems were written as part of a six-part cycle called 'The Z', about ballooning and the rise and fall of the zeppelin industry.

lawn-chair larry
(honorary mention)

larry had bad eyes and never made pilot
larry spent 20 years sulking in his yard
looking at planes overhead

but larry wasn't just an inventor
he was also a vietnam veteran
and a truck driver
and he had an extremely comfortable lawn chair
he bought 45 weather balloons
filled them with helium and called his chair
inspiration one

he made sandwiches for the trip
grabbed a CB radio
and his pellet gun
because larry felt like
calmly ascending to a few dozen feet
floating over his back yard for a couple of hours
and descending again
shooting balloon after balloon
for an extremely calm landing

larry had friends too
after he sat down with his sandwiches
his gun
and his cans of miller lite
they strapped him in
released the anchor
and there went larry
with his balloons
35 cubic feet of helium a piece
cannonballing up into the sky
bye-bye yard bye-bye neighbourhood
hello altitude

larry shot up 300
1,500
3,000 feet
and more
until he'd disappeared
and his dazed friends stopped waving
with larry's glasses at their feet

larry stabilised at some 15,000 feet
where he was too scared to shoot
and the thin air made him dizzy

for 14 hours he drifted scared
but mainly frozen stiff
with his beer and his sandwiches
and his bad eyes
in his extremely comfortable lawn chair
until pilots noticed him
and started discussing him on the radio

after 14 hours he dared to open fire
but lost his gun in the process

slowly
he descended with his balloons
until close to ground level
where he got tangled in power lines

long beach and larry were blacked out
for 20 minutes
munching sandwiches in the dark
until he climbed down
to terra firma
and got cuffed

why did you do it larry walters from L.A.

a man can't just
sit around he said

larry broke an aviation law
though no one knew which one

11 years later larry hitched
to his favourite spot in the woods
put the barrel against his heart
and made his final descent

Larry Walters (1949-1993)

1914-1918 by night

the first city in the world
to be bombed by a Z
was antwerp

in the night of 24 august they came
in early september they came
8 october they came
not once did they bother to aim
progress was just getting started

the germans put it on postcards

    sketches from the front
    hand-coloured

cathedral square with exploding antwerpians

the triumphs of aviation
widened horizons everywhere
our new front was delivered free of charge
the sky

the Z moved the battlefield
from firing line to hinterland
from soldiers to civilians
war had become more total
more honest
                    more fairly distributed

now it overcame you completely
like rain under your skull
it was your own breath that got you
the sky had become a constant enemy
and the sky always came at night

antwerp got off lightly
with death fire and destruction
antwerp was a practice run

rising through occupied sky they came
Z by Z heading for london

in germany the children sang

   fly zeppelin fly
   fly away to london town
   london town is burning down
   fly zeppelin fly

they did
in 1915

one night gigantic lights
searched the skies
they couldn't believe what they found
heavy and silent in their divine peace
the bellies of the Zs hung over them

then came the soft sound of cries
a kind of bellowing
out of nowhere
expectant cries
from the city that had stopped to stare

no traffic no chaos
just 7 million people looking up
in the night
at the gods' silver silence
elongated full moons
packed full

they fired guns
far below them
the ships saw shells explode
it left them cold

on the ground people waited calmly
as if in a beaker
laid out on a catastrophic tray

and up there in the gondolas of the Zs
they said

    release slowly

and it began

the guns forming a sinking
bass line for bombs
the entire city turning into
a lullaby for voice and catacombs

the downside of the night
the downside of an air force in its infancy
is that it's hard to aim properly

the bombs all fell in residential neighbourhoods
the dead were all civilians

in the theatre they heard explosions
an actor said in an ardent aside

    firing practice

he played his role with abandon
and the audience remained seated
while the bodies fell
on pavements and in doorways

the german airships didn't arrive
they were suddenly there
like a downpour

you could play dead or wait or pray
that the god of the tombola was in a good mood
overhead they'd dumped
a load of fluttering butterflies with names written on them
and everyone hoped they were the neighbours'

1916 was a glowing year
the burning bullet was invented
the bullet contained phosphorus P
the Z contained hydrogen H
H and P form a couple
red-hot lovers

when on 2 september
16 Zs glided calmly to london
without a trace of sound
robinson appeared behind one of them
in his heavier than air craft
the aeroplane

this pilot had learnt
to fly as high as the fish gods

robinson fired from his darkness
emptying his magazine of phosphorus
into the tail under the fin
and kept watching
as a pale glow
appeared in the hull of the Z

like a lantern of flesh it spread
as gently as light in a nursery

the tail caught fire
the ship hung in the sky
it hung in the sky

as calm as a burning star
and stayed there

for more than a minute

blazing in graceful silence
the Z slowly started its dive
tipping towards london

where someone burst into god save the king
and another until the gathered city
was singing under german fireworks

high above them
the sky became a waiting room
for 15 other airships
the crews looked on

80 kilometres away a commander scribbled
observations in a logbook

    enormous flame over london
    slowly sinking and growing smaller

and did an about-face
with terror in his gondola

they never carried parachutes
not at the expense of bomb space

from 1916 on
Z after Z went up in flames
they were days of hope

meanwhile somewhere in germany
a man with a cap and moustache died

count Z had been ignored for years
his company had been taken over
he had been barred as a nuisance
he had been forced to sit by grumbling
while his dream was fulfilled
without him

during his funeral
two black Zs suddenly flew over
dropping flowers
flowers
flowers
scattered over germany
in a steady stream
the flowers kept coming
while the coffin sank into the ground
as if the war was sinking with the Zs

but before it got that far
they wanted to try one last thing

it sounded simple:
when problems pile up
germany must go higher

aeroplanes could climb to 4,000 metres
so one day the Z risked it
and discovered 6,000

straight into heaven was the mission
they called them height climbers
as protection against inhuman cold
the crew were advised to line their flying suits
with a solid layer of old newspapers

on the way to the top they lost the war
the news was written in thick black headlines
on their half-frozen bodies

besides their agonies
they were flying too high
for bombing anyway
the ground had dwindled
away to nothing

around them
thermometers burst
compasses went wild
the engines failed one by one

the crew screeched like eagles
a breath away from death

1918 coming up

Becoming
Poet Laureate of the Netherlands

On 28 January 2009, Ramsey Nasr became Poet Laureate of the Netherlands for a term of four years, after a public vote on the poem overleaf.

Its title refers to "Spleen", a famous poem by the Dutch poet Godfried Bomans (after Friedrich Torberg), whose last lines go something like this:

> *I wish I was two little dogs,*
> *then I could play together.*

I wish I was two citizens
(then I could live together)

and this is my poem, come on in
don't be afraid, ignore the echo
let us begin in emptiness
welcome to my crater of light

once we gathered, you and I, remember
revived by the cool gleam of a rummer
our shadows like finest crystal
our fame as glancing as the light that falls
on a letter read by a woman becalmed

we were gold dusted
pale, almost translucent with love
lowering our eyes before each other

and we loved to do penance
if someone asked how we were
we answered truthfully
ashamed to our boots, sir
firmly convinced
that we ourselves had scourged
our very own lord
and crucified him personally
the certainty of the apocalypse
was branded on our retinas

what happened in the few short centuries
we looked the other way?

I hoped to show you a fatherland
formal, pure and with sustained metaphors
moulding a poem about us, but when I began
I had to look on while one nation
spontaneously wiped out the other
like two irreconcilable republics

how did we move so fast from humble to rude
from a glimmer to an omnipresent shrieking crew?
how could careful caterpillars give rise to this hummer tribe?

they say: because god disappeared – our father
had decided to make himself even more invisible
to see if it was possible, no, it wasn't
and god was gone
                        and in this still-life with absentee
the astonished netherlands now stood
mouths full of mortality
full of frivolity and highly regarded death wish

all their vanity had been revealed as vanity
the gleam of them, the dust they embraced
the palace of mirrors people once took for eternity
had been declared unfit for habitation
the frost crackled on their souls

and out of that gap we were born
kevin, ramsey, dunya, dagmar, roman and charity
appearing as if by magic
bungee-jumping, with inflatable orange hammers
screaming and screeching and anti-depressive
or gang-banged in silence for a breezer
a big welcome to the nether regions

yes, that's what you get, this is what's left
when you ram the guilt out of our bodies
we fill the hole with gleaming emptiness

between psalm singing and pill popping
between gold and bling
I found a country where everything must go

this land is the revenge of the forefathers
like an iconoclastic fury they rage on in us
but it exists – like the connection between
burkas and kids' padded bikinis exists
between buttermilk and binge drinking:
concave and convex our centuries slide together

cancelling each other out is our strength
our nature strives for emptiness
like a cyclops longs for depth

you see, I wanted to show you a fatherland
not this desert of infinite freedom
but this is where we live
and how beautiful it would be
if someone one day like a second-hand deity
could build a country rhyme by rhyme
for this nation that misses its nation

here of all places, in the open pit of our heart
we can achieve something great
a poem's a start

Poems written in the function of
Poet Laureate of the Netherlands

Shortly after having been chosen as the new Poet Laureate of the Netherlands, Ramsey Nasr received a request to write a poem on the occasion of a new Vermeer exhibition. It was an exhibition of one painting only, "Woman Holding a Balance", courtesy of The National Gallery of Art in Washington. The empty balancing dishes, the gold and the pearls on the table, the mysterious lady and the picture of Doomsday behind her all reminded Nasr of the front pages of those weeks: the news of the economic crisis and the collapse of the economy.

What's Left
A poem about empty dishes

Imagine a room. The room contains a number of regular elements.
There is a window on the left. There is the light it admits. A pearl
                                                                    necklace
and a yellow satin coat with an ermine collar. Invariably there is a table
to display the elements: look, a loaf of bread; look, a basket.
These are the organs.

Adorning the back of the room is a painting or a map. At least, a nail.
Then the canvas is gone for a moment, standing behind the observer.
Painting, window, mirror and map form the boundaries
a second skin to live in. A miraculous membrane breathing
between inside and out.

Only the visitors change. They move the organs now and then
stand motionless in their closed systems of paint and sable hairs
open the window, play lute or guitar, read letters, pour milk
or stand in the Dutch room, all warm gravidity.
Like this lady.

With her belly before her like a glowing sickle
she seems to weigh air. She is expectant. But of what?
The woman is not weighing, she is waiting. Like some kind of Mary
wrapped in the night's pouch of blue and white. Unapproachable
heart with two dishes.

People see her for much that she is not. They used to say,
"Vanitas. The woman is pondering eternal life." They called her
Woman Weighing Gold. Or Pearls. Her belly a crowded room full.
It was the gleam that misled us like aureoles, for centuries.
Because the dishes are empty.

And those who seek references, want deep-sea insights or cherish
higher values should do just that, but this is enough.
For me this is sufficient, like a pagan faith in the tangible.
The sublime resides in this room. A crust is a window is a table.
Vermeer was the great equaliser.

When the painter died, he left the organs intact:
the glass, the paintings, the map and also the yellow coat
that had been worn by one woman and then another
they were still there in the room, which seemed no emptier than usual.
Only the master was gone.

Not a sketch or drawing of him remained, today we know
virtually nothing, no diary excerpts or chance letters
except the letters on his paintings, that have since been spread
over The Hague, Amsterdam, Berlin, Paris, New York and Washington.
The room has multiplied.

2.

There is another room as well. This room is scarcely lit.
Nothing on the table. It is quiet and deserted. The window
is round and tiny. A peephole through which the world
looked in, casting a sky-blue colour on the wall.
This was the boardroom.

From here loans were handed out for years like so many pearls.
Passing the readies to anyone able to mist a mirror or sign
on the line unaided while meanwhile they tried to keep the pearl
or at least withhold the gleam so they could flog it again later
on a separate occasion,

by transferring it to a new room, where they could chisel
the weight away from the gleam to deliberately lay it on
someone else's table as their holy credit rating, over and over
on someone else's hopeful table – risk has to move, move away, fast
out of this room, further still

from room to room, until in the last pitch-black corner
the shadow of the weight of the gleam of the former pearl was also
removed, and the caboodle repacked so many times the walls began
to slide and tunnels formed of their own accord like bundles of nerves
in a system with no exit.

And the system
saw that it was good

neither head nor tail
uncentred excessive

it was lighter than ether
better than perfect.

Its only reference self-referential
it became more and more multipliable. It spread across
the waters in expanding ecstasy as a sky-blue light, from New York
to Paris, Berlin and The Hague, Amsterdam – until finally
no one was able to distinguish a mirror from a window.

Technically speaking things were going
peachy. Casting aside moralism even cancer
can be seen as a chivalrous form of reproduction
unadulterated profit in fact. We were overrun with prosperity.
It was just a downer when someone asked about the pearl necklace.

The pearls… yeah. Where had they got to?
They were crushed and spread, love, like glittering confetti
somewhere on the edges of our economy. But where exactly,
that is the question. And the woman asked once more about her pearls.
Two dishes in her hand. Outside, like a lump of twilight, the sun began
to set.

In Washington, basking in her lead yellow glow
the lady had waited and waited. Now she watched
as the dishes gradually came to a standstill, as before her eyes
in a sudden equilibrium of thin air and deliberate hot air the whole
system collapsed like a punctured lung – room after room after room.

3.

I have a suggestion.
It's time to count our blessings. Milk. Earrings.
Delft bricks. We are the owners of light. Like good
trustees we should feed ourselves again with paint.

That's not difficult.
You take a shockproof container to America and ask,
"The orange curtain, that light from the left and that pair of old dishes
can we borrow them? In a couple of months we'll bring it all back."

But we won't.
That canvas is staying here. We're going to dismantle
and bring back every room. We'll reassemble the lot and
sit down in that one room. Calmly counting what's left.

This is what's left:
one mirror. Two hands. Black-and-white floor, golden edges
glowing sickle and ultramarine. The cinders of a catastrophe
are as tangible as bread or glass. As edible as a table.

This at least – this is real.
Let the pregnant woman stay here, in this building. Not out of greed
but to save our lives. We gave them the gleam of a pearl as a pledge.
That will have to do. To each his own.

We were screwed right down the line
wrung out to the bone we lived in boxes of optical illusion
but that paint is ours. Today we will learn to look. Let us
cut back in this room, and grow accustomed to the lean years.

Let us use the very last
bonuses we have left, scraped up out of the shameless
chinks of our souls, to get our canvases back and say
That is bread. This is stained glass. And that's the feel of the glitter of
water.

It's not too late.
Look through the window from outside to in. Go on, look: it says
what it says. And yes, that's not much. But we too will be rich.
We will learn to take pride in owning empty dishes.

In May 2009 an exhibition called "Calvin and Us" opened in the Dordrecht Minster, where William of Orange publicly declared himself a Calvinist in 1573.

Ramsey Nasr opened the exhibition by reciting from the pulpit a newly written psalm about Calvin's influence on the Dutch people. He did this before an audience that included the Dutch queen and many theologians and ministers from all over the country. The poem, **psalm for an origin**, raised a small scandal in the Calvinist community.

psalm for an origin

god of the house of orange

the fathers say
I can address you directly
no saints as go-betweens
but directly, hence this prayer
without form or frippery

the fathers say:

>   we went looking for him
>   and returned
>   ink-black and cast down
>   humbled before him

>   we roared when our hearts broke
>   whitewashed our walls
>   razed and blasted the body
>   closed our openings

I asked, why?
and the fathers said:

because we wanted
to live our lives towards him, unscathed
spare and lean, each himself
a letter in his sight

only the mouth
opening at appropriate times
as a quiver for our astonishment
or ignorance, and also for psalms
telescoping a solitary voice
to reach him in isolation

and I asked, where?
and the fathers said:

he lives on the edge of the approachable
but his light is upon us
legibility is true life

there they stand
sealed until the day of days
skin and flesh consumed
almost abstract in the purity of their form
waiting for his meticulous wrath

the fathers say that out of love
you built a body to work against them
piling gall and difficulties around them
and in this desperation they find solace

but god of my origin
that body of theirs
is strange to me
inhabited by strangers

they are practised in death
I have a weakness for life

maybe it's true
that I was born of evil
and thrived on injury
squatting between stains and calumny
in my field of blossoming desire

but I fear
my tongue has a mind for malice
and speaks like a razor
because I do not know my aberrations

I may love the words that devour
and rant as I stray
but tell me if you can
how can I sin
if I have never learned to sin?

I am a splinter of my origin
and possibly doomed
risen from a sulphured womb
but here I stand

incapable of any good
inclined to all evil
cut free of god and gods

and the fathers do not speak of me
and no one rules over me
but no one tears me from their hand

I eat their bread
but it is my skin that glows like an oven
and from the burning of their sins
I still drink the sweat of their fear

here perhaps, in this shame
we come together, in this blushing midway
between bare disbelief and solid despair
we find each other

the fathers and I
orphans under one sky

as pious persecutors of the flesh
they have lived according to the letter
down to the bare bones

but I
I cannot go deeper than this
I want a body

stripped and thin
as a mondrian tree
I've led my life for years
between tongues and chalices
drowning in flowers
incapable of giving myself over
to anything except this shame

god of orange
wherever you are
give me a body
because this can't go on

I am full of troubles
in desperation I have tried
to violently tear down

your dark-black rules
until one by one I could open
my stuttering senses
until I could suddenly hear and see
and with pores dilated
could snort and pop
at every opening
making up for what was lost.

I have broken the seals
entirely reformed this body of mine
seceded from you

call it a rebellion of the flesh
an act of abandonment

but still no body
and now I am invisible too:
completely naked and transparent

here I stand
with my empty brand-new body
in which everything, everything is public
nothing could be left unspeakable
and here, with this funnel of a soul
I call to you

I call to you
with all of my reluctance
wind-blasted, unwalled inside and out:

if you want to be my god of origin
give me somewhere to start

again the fathers say:

> he lives on the edge of the approachable
> he knows when we sit and when we stand up
> he surrounds us when we go and feels when we lie
>   down
> he walks our paths with us

well god, if that's true
then I know where to find you
even if I've never looked

full of disbelief
I have felt you in me for years
aching and throbbing, uninvited
you rise up in an extra row of molars
just like that, unjustified, for no reason
or I feel you sitting by aimlessly
at the end of an appendix
just sitting there, completely forgotten
an unused tonsil or earlobes
idle and indolent

but this is your day
oh, god of the coccyx

if you must hang round
enflame properly

raise your right hand
swell in me with all your strength
tear me out now or break my bones to pieces
but do something, god

drive this body together
make it run like a herd
I need a body

the fathers say that we can't alter
a hair of our salvation
but hear me now, for I shall rise

surrounded by colour and voluptuous curves
I will go around as in an oriental city
in the quarters and alleys of my flesh I will seek
and if I find you – take shelter, god
because I will not let go
not before I have forced you
to lock the doors of the inside rooms
and draw me in behind your hand
so that we can pour out our names

come not as the north or south wind
to blow through my courtyard
do not come upon me as poetry
but break in, do it, deep and ungentle
beat me insensible with furious passion
come upon me as a silent guardian
a beast with burning spices
a farmhand if necessary
but do something

my temples are two bursting pomegranates
my throat is a pounding tower of blood
because this heart is tempestuous
my hands drip with desire
ten fingers are liquid myrrh around you
and around the heavy handle of your bolt

rise in me, god
make me swell like the early fruit of the fig
gather me in, open my waiting skin
stand up in me as in your first love
my beauty, my blossoming
I will pray with my legs
come to me as a fragrant rod
and be kind to me in this new form
as the tender vines give off their scent

come now, god
I am black but I can be comely
I carry the promise of unity in me

come
so I can grasp my errors
so I can embrace myself
so I can walk together
with the sparkling beast in my bones

this fortress of hair and flesh
this citadel of former shame
I will now make it my home
I will keep this body

this reptilian brain will steer me
yearning and steaming
taking me up in one clear line
through millions of distant fathers
back to the core

I know you are there
you are inside me like a hopeful monster
my beautiful infinite code of letters
and I will multiply for you
halving myself time after time, from love
splintering into others and being diluted again
because I will bring forth new species

I will strut around you like the graceful gazelle
sing for you like a lyrebird
learn to writhe like a salamander
dance and float like a sea pen

my mouth is most sweet
I am lovely in all things

my love is for you and you alone
my god of origin, accept me

I carry a strange beast in my breast
bastardised by nature and essentially unclean

but that beast is me and no one else
can lightly free me from all sin

3 Sonnets

400 years ago, in September 1609, a Dutch East India Company ship sailed into an unknown bay on the North American coast. Captain Henry Hudson hoped to find a shorter, northern route to the Indies, instead he stumbled upon a territory that would be populated in the years that followed by Dutch merchants and colonists, eventually developing into the most renowned city in the world: New Amsterdam, later New York.

The 400th anniversary of Dutch–American relations was celebrated in the Choir Church in Middelburg on 2 September 2009 in the presence of Princess Margriet, the U.S. ambassador and the Dutch Minister of Foreign Affairs, Maxime Verhagen.

On the invitation of the Roosevelt Study Center, as Poet Laureate of the Netherlands, Ramsey Nasr wrote the three following sonnets, which he recited during the ceremony.

1 – Hudson's Shortcut

our outcome was that you were in the way
we sailed to that conclusion on a dream
dreamt by a fool: our captain hudson claimed
that he could find a shortcut to the east

go straight and keep the north pole on your left
then you can slip down quickly to the indies
and we believed the guy and followed him
yes, even when he said: "or maybe west...?"

henry hudson had been dismissed before
and when he swore on the shore of a foreign bay
that all we had to do to reach the orient
was set a course straight through america
we'd wisely lowered sail – already wedged
from stem to stern in this new continent

2 – New Amsterdam

the waiting bay lay like an outstretched finger
at the end of an invisible dutch arm
we went exploring, stamping round we found
our way in a deserted fertile backwater

perhaps no other body but ours, which never
managed to win one god, one people for itself
which rose from drifting, loose minorities
could lay the seed for such a babelopolis

who taught you how to use the melting pot?
who said, be equal, be diverse and free
your trade, who told you, dreams can spread like shares?
the true world champions of immigration
we were, a distant spark of liberty
america, the netherlands writ small

3 – New Netherland

oh font of humanism, oh shining beacon
oh cradle of exemplary citizenship
who listens to us now? we have our leaders
they blare their christian values round the place
and mount the moralistic foghorn high
but in america their frightened faces
all gleam with drooling pride, it's not prime time
but still we steal a slot in the cool white house

what kind of model country toes this line?
we bob along behind the big boss boat
impressive, don't you think? a fifty-state fleet
with an inspiring airbed at the back
WANTED URGENTLY: foolish fools with vision
who dare to dream and make the cold sea crack

January 2010 saw the publication of the Davids Commission report on its enquiry into the Dutch government's decision to support the Iraq war. Jan Peter Balkenende was the Dutch prime minister both when the report was released and earlier when the Dutch government supported the war.

New Year's Greetings

So JP, how's it feel to tell a lie
and see it surface later as a headline?
How does it feel, as a Christian-Democrat,
to have come down on the side of Herod,

killing hundreds of thousands of children
for just one king? International law?
I know a country that's ignored a dozen
resolutions for years with our support.

That's our PM, he reads the morning paper,
sighs, and thinks to himself: what a palaver.
My conscience is clear. No wheat without chaff.

Besides, a lie is always white when patriotic.
Belated season's greetings from the people of Iraq,
liberated into graves and destroyed en masse.

Heavenly Life
(Mahler 4)

This lyrical epic was written to commemorate the
hundred and fiftieth anniversary of Gustav Mahler's
birth and is based on his Fourth Symphony, with
the sections of the poem echoing the structure,
tone and length of its movements.

The poem is named after "Das himmlische Leben",
the song that forms the symphony's finale. It deals
with the deep relationship between Mahler, the
Dutch conductor Mengelberg and the Royal
Concertgebouw Orchestra over a period of about
fifty years.

I

Bedächtig. Nicht eilen – Recht gemächlich

In the distance: the sound of approaching sleighs, brass bells
     gliding through the landscape. Over the snowy hills
     they come, like in a Bohemian fairy tale, descending.
It is 1901. A century awakes. Wintry themes glide past,
     linking up together, moving from flute and lingering
     clarinet to high strings, then back down to the double
     basses and horns, returning to the clarinet. The first
     melodies dance in a circle without being fully
     developed. Unbothered, they form a carefree swarm of
     fresh lines, driven together by bells, a herd of
     impatient children.
Snow falls from the milky sky.
Between the sleighs, a little giant strides by, walking stick in
     hand. His magnificent domed forehead hangs over the
     sparkling eyes behind his round glasses. Gustav Mahler
     composes outdoors. He leaps over rocks, climbing and
     wandering from key to key.
Now he stands still. He looks up at the feathery crystals that
     are falling down into his hand and wanders on, leaving
     a trail in the snow as he winds his way to 1902.

Hundreds of kilometres away, in a city in northern Europe, a
     young man spreads his arms before an orchestra. Now
     and then he speaks to it, this fabled beast of wood,

brass, strings and skin. And the newborn beast listens,
producing music when he waves his hand.
Soon, the cub has a sound of its own. Willem Mengelberg shapes
it like a general. His concerts are a fight to the death.

a titanic struggle
in which humans
can achieve
the superhuman

Meanwhile Mahler has wandered on to Germany. He stops just
short of the Dutch border – it is 1902 – enters a full hall
and starts to conduct one of his symphonies. After one and
a half hours the music ends where the Fourth just began: a
children's choir sings like a heavenly carillon and bells ring.
Cymbals, tambourines, small drums sound from the
various balconies. In the hall, light snow begins to fall.
Mengelberg is there. Afterwards he watches the sweating
conductor with the round glasses, seeing him turn on the
podium to greet the snow-covered audience, gesturing
ecstatically at his children's choir.
Today the two men meet. They become friends.

1903. Invited by Mengelberg, Mahler strolls into the
Netherlands. For the first time his music is heard in the
Concertgebouw. The composer conducts – and is totally
enthused by both orchestra and audience.

this country is astonishing
the applause was deafening

the audiences here
are all ear

It wasn't like that everywhere. At the premiere of his fourth
symphony the baffled audience remained seated. No one
understood what the little giant was trying to say: such
perverse naivety, so fragmented and so absolutely
contradictory... Where was the heroism? The jubilant
purity? What kind of finale was that?
The sweetest of all his symphonies had frightened them in
Germany.

For the Dutch premiere of the Fourth, Mengelberg invites the
composer back to the Netherlands – here comes Mahler
strolling up again – and promptly tells him the best way
to let an audience adjust to the unprecedented.

sunday evening
concertgebouw

gustav mahler
symphony no. 4

interval

gustav mahler
symphony no. 4

Mahler beams. In Mengelberg he has found, for the first
time, a friend who really understands his music: a
world like an overcrowded head, inhabited by Medieval
mystics, bumbling brass bands and oriental
philosophers, klezmer musicians, travellers, angels and
children.
The composer will return to Amsterdam often. He feels at
home here and calls Amsterdam his second fatherland.
Still, around this time, his lover receives a melting letter:

I wasn't born to be a nomad
it's a terrible life this
hanging round abroad

no matter how loving the welcome
one is thwarted on all sides
and finally abandoned

In the year of the Fourth it stops snowing. The instruments
that couldn't count to three before, now produce wider
arches, rising from the strings and descending in the
other sections. They're the same melodies as just now,
but developed into limbs.
The orchestra reaches puberty. There are protests against
Mengelberg and his high-handed authoritarianism.

135

Wood, brass, gut and skin demand a say. Eleven of
them are fired, others automatically fill the empty
chairs. Mengelberg is Herr im Hause. He raises a
hand: the sound of bells rises from the body.

And then there's disease. And then there is death. Flowers,
flowers and more flowers bury the cemetery.
Hundreds of wreaths, while icy rain pours down on
all present. The little giant strolls no more. He is lying
under the ground next to a four-year-old girl.
Eternally four, his favourite daughter.

gustav mahler
(1860-1911)

Mengelberg takes the young symphonies under his wing like
an orphaned family. More determined than ever, he
performs Mahler, letting his friend stand on his own
two feet.
Successfully, for now. The Fourth is on the programme for
the remembrance concert. Loud applause sounds after
the final movement – but after the first movement too
and after the adagio. As if they're trying to clap him
back. Flakes of snow drift down from the balconies.

In 1920 Mengelberg organises an homage to his friend,
celebrating his 25th anniversary at the
Concertgebouw by performing the complete Mahler

in two weeks with his orchestra. This titanic task forms
the first international music festival since the end of the
world war. Composers, conductors, musicians, they
come from all over Europe with a single dream: peace
and brotherhood between nations and countries.
Neutral Holland is the perfect setting for this dream.
Mahler's music is its embodiment.

Mengelberg is now generally adored. He is more popular
than Queen Wilhelmina. Under his hand the orchestra
comes to life. "The boss" is still his nickname, but he's
actually a king, borne on the shoulders of the
fatherland.

Everywhere the sound of bells. A sickly sweet smell drifts
through the streets of Amsterdam. A solitary magic
horn heralds something and here it comes: extremely
slowly the trees blossom in a floral version of the
opening theme. Spring has arrived.
Completely unexpectedly, one last gust of wind comes out of
nowhere to accelerate and accelerate and finally burst
into a whirlwind of instruments playing together. Tutti,
fortissimo.

All the chestnuts are in blossom. It is 1933. The sun breaks
through and Germany has a new chancellor.

II

In gemächlicher Bewegung. Ohne Hast

The concertmaster, at the front of the stage on the left,
tunes his violin, setting all four strings one tone
higher. The other musicians watch, waiting.
When the concertmaster nods, the man on the podium
raises his arm, holding the baton like a gentle club.
The horn strikes up a restless melody. Three-eight
time: uproar in the forest.
At the water's edge the frog blares his gossip at the polecat, a
beetle complains about the squirrel's stench. Other
animals join in. A heron approaches without being
seen. A bear listens, standing by stupidly. Like a big
drum it peers jealously at the timpani while above
them the scolding cuckoos defend their branch from
the owl.
And shrieking through it all is the first violin. Shrill and
scratchy, that was how the little giant wanted it here,
like the folk music he heard as a child, like pale death
in a fairy tale.
All the creatures are now talking at the same time,
incomprehensible in their wood, brass, gut and skin,
until a burly harp with flowing blonde hair appears.
She has the solution. Naked she dances from tree to
tree and disappears. The forest follows in a waltzing

procession. One by one, a long line of waltzing
animals and bushes.
It's the great depression.

The Concertgebouw languishes in the lean years. The mood
is sombre.
Not Mengelberg's. In the spring of 1933 he tours Italy,
where he meets the Italian fascist leader. The
conversation is pleasant and the conductor notes
cheerfully that Mussolini's love of music is boundless.

1935, October. In Berlin the Nuremberg Race Laws are in
force. To keep the German race pure, sex between
Aryans and Jews has been forbidden. Mixed marriages
are annulled. To preserve what has been built up.
Mengelberg receives an invitation to conduct in Berlin and
is keen to accept. His enthusiasm for Germany does
not go down well. Rumours circulate that hundreds
upon hundreds of subscribers have cancelled their
season tickets out of protest.
Mengelberg persists, hoping to conduct Mahler in Berlin –
the city where performing or listening to Jewish
music is illegal and where the Mahlerstrasse has just
lost its name.

1936, March. On the Dutch radio a prime minister speaks
to his nation, reassuring the fatherland: everyone can
sleep calmly. In the background, harp music.

Later that year a journalist tells Mengelberg that in Leipzig
    they've knocked down the statue of Mendelssohn.
    Mendelssohn is a Jew. And Mengelberg gets angry.
    You shouldn't believe all you hear about Germany.
The lights dim early in some homes. In the glow of the
    moon, a slow waltz passes by.

When the Concertgebouw Orchestra is invited to tour
    Germany in 1937, various members refuse. But
    Mengelberg is the boss. He declares:

I am an artist
and an artist must not
get involved with politics

art is above all parties
like the sun, it is created
to shine on all races

He reproaches the Jews in his orchestra for not wanting to
    go. Germany is the chance of a lifetime and the boss
    personally guarantees their safety. He can't understand
    musicians having the gall to take a political position.
    It is their duty to remain neutral and reconcile others.

In 1938, after the Anschluss, the Mahlerstrasse in Vienna is
    renamed too and the little giant's bust is removed
    from the opera he once ran.

Flutes and piccolos twitter in the bushes, a slow waltz moves
   on through the forest until the forest itself has
   disappeared, behind the others.

1939, October. The Concertgebouw's new music season
   opens. The programme includes Das Lied von der
   Erde. Composer: Gustav Mahler. Mengelberg has
   cancelled and stays in his chalet in Switzerland. The
   German Carl Schuricht conducts in his place.

The moving final song Der Abschied is sung by Kerstin
   Thorborg, a mezzo-soprano who fled Vienna a year
   before to escape the Nazis:

   the earth breathes
   full of rest and sleep
   all longings want to dream

   the birds perch motionless
   on their branches
   the world is falling asleep

   oh, beauty
   oh, drunken world

Thorborg falls silent. She sits down and listens to the long
   orchestral interlude until the orchestra, too, gradually
   falls silent. And then, on this ecstatic pedal note – it

happens. A lady in one of the front rows stands up and calmly walks up to the stage until she is close to the singer and conductor. Calmly and loudly she informs the maestro:

deutschland über alles, herr schuricht

The acoustics of the Concertgebouw are too perfect to leave the song unscathed. The lady exits in a shrieking silence.

Schuricht doesn't speak. The full house doesn't speak. Only Mahler's double basses growl on quietly, scarcely audible, like a sustained deep note in the pathless forest.

Actually there wasn't any silence: after a second the orchestra, exposed on its bare plain, simply plays on. With a wave of a deathly pale hand, the woodwinds pick up the theme, a tempo. The brass follows. And the song of the earth resumes its course as prescribed.

Only the people have been damaged.

In the hall, apart from all this and sounding like it's coming from some other place:

where I am going?
I go. I wander up mountains
seeking rest for my lonely heart

the dear earth
everywhere on all sides
blossoming in spring
shooting up like always

everywhere on all sides
and eternally blue
horizons loom up

eternally...
eternally...

eternally blue...

Here and there the pinging of a celesta.
At some stage a farewell is made. From now on, everything
    is memory.

Leaving the Concertgebouw, the audience sees sixteen
    sleighs. No one knows where they have come from.
    There are no children, no rolling hills. There is no
    forest, no fairy tale. There is just the city and sixteen
    empty waiting sleighs.
Passers-by stop to look up. Big flakes fall down in the form
    of luminescent stars with a word written on every
    star. The same word over and over. Four melting

letters. Everyone looks at the blue sky but the stars are hanging from the branches, dropping to the ground, sticking to random passers-by.

The new season has begun.

III

Ruhevoll (poco adagio)

The most beautiful adagio Mahler ever wrote. On a
   passacaglia plucked out by the bass players, a melody
   comes floating in, completely disengaged, with the
   strings. First the cellos.
The air in the theatre is sluggish. Everything seems frozen in
   an unreal calm.

Rotterdam has been reduced to rubble. Mengelberg is in
   Germany. People say he drank champagne with the
   Germans. Even before the port has stopped
   smouldering, a request for free tickets for German
   officers arrives at the Concertgebouw.
Violas pick up the theme. Gently they take the ends of the
   floating melody and play with it in counterpoint,
   together with a few cellos.

During the bombing the Rotterdam Philharmonic's library,
   concert hall and rehearsal rooms were destroyed,
   along with many of its instruments. Twenty-six
   members of the orchestra have lost everything.
   Rotterdam has lost itself. The Netherlands has lost its
   leaders. The Concertgebouw organises a benefit.
Without the boss, the podium is empty and abandoned –
   but here conductors are not necessary. The second

violins start automatically, a tenth higher, varying
freely on the cello's themes.

In July 1940 Mengelberg is photographed in Berlin,
together with his wife. Smiling at a poster
announcing a performance by the Berlin
Philharmonic. Conductor: Willem Mengelberg.
The first violins join in. They repeat the opening theme,
several octaves higher, rarefied, rising. Adding layers
of bliss one after the other. Supported by the rhythm
of the double basses, the cellos rise, the violas push
off, the second violins come off the ground and the
first violins ascend, one by one, coming together in a
mist. They disappear, the concertmaster leading the
way.
He disappears first.

Sam Swaap is a former member of the Concertgebouw
Orchestra. In the summer of 1940 he leads the first
violins of the Residency Orchestra. There, in The
Hague, after the concert, the Jew makes a mistake: he
accepts the conductor's outstretched hand.

mr. swaap's
music stand
was moved slightly
to the rear

And the Jew played on, less visibly. Not shrieking like
death, but like a man in a fairy tale. In highly civilised
's-Gravenhage.

Mengelberg is back in the Netherlands for a few days. He
has booked a room at the Amstel Hotel and let the
German Reich Commissioner know that he can
expect him. It seems the Nazi is very passionate about
music.
Upon arrival, Mengelberg declares his love for Germany.
He wonders what's wrong with that.

Somewhere else the musicians stroll in one after the other.
Instead of sitting down on the waiting chairs, they
move on, already playing their instruments, to the
other rooms, floating on their slow passacaglia.

Mengelberg puts Mahler on the programme for the concert
season '40/'41. The Reich Commissioner is
astounded by so much naivety – and a little angry too.
He gives permission for one last performance of a
single work by the Jew, to mark the end of an era.
The board has no wish to provoke the occupier and
withdraws the request. Only Mengelberg insists. The
boss wants to play Mahler for as long as possible. And
the Reich Commissioner said they can.
This new musical friend has a proposal of his own. It's called
"purging the orchestral body". And anyone who

persists in performing Jewish works can forget about
any subsidies. The Concertgebouw gets to choose.

For the last performance of Mahler, four members of the
        orchestra are given new places. Seated at the front of
        the stage, the Jews were all too visible.
It's a wonderful concert.

In the week that follows there is a celebration in the
        Concertgebouw. The first cheerful evening since the
        outbreak of war. The hall is enchanting, decorated
        with banners and red, white and blue flags.
        Enormous letters loom up behind the orchestra:

joy and work
arts for the people

At the press conference several days earlier, Mengelberg said:

art is a sun
that must shine for all people

people have an essential need
to dwell in an ideal atmosphere

I think what you are doing is magnificent
I've striven for something similar
you can always count on me

Tonight all the music lovers are present: the Reich
   Commission, the SS, the Wehrmacht, the Nazi Party,
   the Dutch National Socialist Movement and many
   sons of the fatherland.
The orchestra plays.

And somewhere, in that other place, the slow passacaglia is
   still audible, like an extracorporeal body. There, too,
   the most moving note Mahler ever wrote now
   blossoms. Out of nowhere the first violins strike up a
   radiant high D and hold it for seconds, minutes, a
   sustained D that breaks through walls, spreading over
   Amsterdam, as light as a feather, skimming over the
   heads of its inhabitants, circling in the free air and
   finally shooting off. One note: like a siren's song it
   pushes through to that other place.
During this heavenly D all members of Dutch orchestras
   have been presented with a form. Form A is for
   Aryans. Form B is for Jews and those who have
   mixed with Jews.
A simple calculation reveals that sixteen Jews are concealed
   in the orchestral body: twelve string players, three
   members of the wind section and one harpist. By the
   end of 1941 the orchestra must be purged of the very
   last Jew.

Mengelberg is shocked. Partly because the orchestra won't
survive a blow like this. The boss manages to get a
temporary reprieve for three Jews: Ben Meijer, Jacques
Muller and Sam Brill. The least Jewish-looking Jews.

An ethereal D is still skimming over the basso ostinato, in
unreal calm. But that is somewhere outside this place,
in a different theatre.

Coming up to the summer of 1941 the last concert with
Jews takes place. Beethoven's Ninth.

divine spark, so heavenly
twilight drunken and rejoicing
we enter your sanctuary

There is no official presentation, no farewell speech has been
prepared. Everything proceeds without a whisper. The
choir beams, all men become brothers. And the
orchestra plays. Thirteen of them have grown
transparent. In their thoughts they have already joined
that divine rarefied D, somewhere less visible. They
move on to that other place to take their seats in the
great orchestra of distance.
Only their bodies are still sitting there, like the glow of
distant stars, while everyone plays on. And as that
rarefied note stretches forth, the jubilation in the
concert hall continues:

let all who have succeeded
in proving friendship for their friends
add their voice to our rejoicing
jubilation, pure and loud

and the others who have failed
weep their silent tears alone
leaving our fraternity

follow, brothers, this your path
that leads you to the arms of millions

up above the starry heavens
a dear father surely dwells

he must dwell above the stars
follow, brothers, this your path

Now the finale has faded away there is only the concert hall.
The choir stands upright, silent. Orchestra and soloists sit
    before them, silent. Facing the silent audience.
Once the applause erupts, it seems to go on forever. The
    audience refuses to stop clapping. They wave
    handkerchiefs. People embrace. Tears fall in the
    Concertgebouw.

leon rudelsheim	*1st violin, 2nd concertmaster — jew*
jo hekster	*1st violin, 3rd concertmaster — jew*
sam tromp	*2nd violin — jew*
sal snijder	*2nd violin — jew*
louis pens	*2nd violin — jew*
simon furth	*2nd violin — jew*
jacques koen	*2nd violin — jew*
sieg de boer	*2nd violin — jew*
simon gompertz	*double bass — jew*
louis salomons	*bassoon — jew*
joseph sloghem	*trumpet — jew*
emanuel haagman	*trombone — jew*
rosa spier	*harp — jewess*

follow, brothers, this your path
that leads you to the arms of millions

In the dressing rooms, instrument cases click shut. The Jews
   pack their bags and, with a peculiar rustling sound,
   leave through the back door.
Ready for the orchestra of distance.
When the door closes, a dying high D finally falls, sliding
   down to a G and lying there motionless. In the
   silence that follows the three least-Jewish-looking
   Jews are sent off on holiday, then fired.
The orchestral body has been purged and takes up the
   heavenly theme once again. A passacaglia for strings,
   as detached as ever.

Life goes on. If necessary, without Jews.

Not much later the remaining members of the orchestra
   receive an enormous pay rise. Government subsidies
   also rise steeply. All thanks to a Dutch Nazi with
   power and a soft spot for music. The years of
   depression are over. Behind the clouds the sun is
   shining.
Russian, Polish, British and American music is no longer
   allowed. And with French works limited to a
   maximum of one piece per concert, these are great
   days for domestic composers. Many geniuses emerge:
   they win state prizes and haul in commission after
   commission. Music is booming.

After the Dutch Chamber of Culture opens in 1942,
   membership remains voluntary. Those who do not
   join are no longer allowed to perform or have their
   compositions performed. From now on, everything is
   harmonised.

Except in one place. Invisible and inaudible to the
   fatherland, forbidden melodies resound in the heart of
   Amsterdam. Deep inside a theatre, they are playing
   Mahler's Fourth. Admission for Jews only. The
   conductor is a Jew. A Jewess sits ready for the final
   song. The bass players pluck a slow passacaglia to rise
   above it all.

The idea comes from the Nazis. As an intermediary solution
they've brought all of the Netherlands' dismissed
Jewish orchestra members together in a new
orchestra.
The final solution will follow in June 1942. That's when
they will start using this theatre to gather Jews before
deporting them to the extermination camps.
Until then they can listen to Mahler. Art is a sun that shines
for all people.

Summer has set in with a vengeance. When traces of Jews
are detected in the Concertgebouw after all –
portraits of the race are hanging in the corridors and
the letters M-A-H-L-E-R are even visible in a place
of honour under the royal balcony – the board passes
a motion to "freshen up the whole series".
They erase Mendelssohn, Rubinstein and Mahler from the
cartouches.
Sand-blasting every corner, up to the horizon.

As the war proceeds, the concerts attract bigger and bigger
crowds. There are full houses every night. The
audiences crave music like bread and water.
The members of the orchestra see their salaries raised again.
In this, the last year of the war, they are exempt from
forced labour and safe from arrest during police raids.
The board does its very best, lending a helping hand
when it can. And resisting when permitted. Thanks to

the orchestra's efforts, all of the Jewish members of
the orchestra survive the war – except for three: a
violinist, a violist and a bass player die in the camps.
They can proceed to the heavenly life.

And, as if responding to a random wave of a hand, a
cloudless sky rustles open, an enormous jubilant
surface in E major, fortissimo, like a trap door going
up. All of the strings whirl up, ascending suddenly to
the heights. Kettledrums and trombones. Blue
horizons, everywhere on all sides.
And then – rest.
Nothing left but liquid harmonies for strings and harp,
gliding open, overlapping, sweet and scented.

Let us now float from one place to the next, serene and free,
heading for the transparent membrane. Let us lay our
hands against it and push through to that other place,
tumbling towards an orchestra in the distance.

Somewhere behind us, Holland is liberated.

IV

Sehr behaglich

We have reached the finale, a vast landscape to believe in.
    The trees are hung with smoked sausages, good
    people ride around on sleighs, angels bake the bread.
    Let us wander around with those who are left. The
    members of the orchestra are standing in a
    magnificent circle, surrounding us like petals.
As naive as a child, a soprano sings:

> *enjoying the pleasures of heaven*
> *we have shunned the earth*
> *the tumult of the world*
> *does not reach us in heaven*
> *our lives here are mild and restful*
>
> *we lead the life of angels*
> *free from troubles, almost living*
> *and all the saints look on*

Far below us, in heaven's basement, a wooden house in the
    countryside. Rolling hills. Trees drop their dry leaves.
    A man with a furrowed brow stands on the balcony.
    He looks up. Rain is in the air.

Mengelberg spent little time in Holland during the last years
of the war. Generally he was either at his Swiss chalet
or touring occupied Europe, conducting orchestras in
Germany, Austria, Italy, Spain and so on. Many
conductors had fled Nazi Europe. There was a
shortage of people who could perform music at the
highest level. Mengelberg alleviated that shortage.
At the start of one of his last Dutch concerts, it remained
deathly still as he descended the steps in the
Concertgebouw. At the bottom he looked at the
audience and said:

if you won't clap for me
do it for the orchestra

After liberation there was a new purge. Nine members of
the orchestra were dismissed for collaborating with
the Germans. Again the wheat was separated from the
chaff.
And a soprano sings:

all kinds of good plants
grow in heaven's garden
good beans and asparagus
good apples, grapes and pears

Mengelberg looks up, a gentle drizzle starts to fall. On the
roof of his chalet is a lyre, a wooden copy of the lyre
that adorns the façade of the Concertgebouw.
Mengelberg will never take up the baton again. He
will never return to the Netherlands. He has been
found guilty of ruthless conducting. The prolongation
of beauty in the years of death. He dies in neutral
Switzerland, broken and completely misunderstood.

I never did anything against my fatherland
I was always a loyal subject
whatever I did or did not do
it was directly or indirectly
for the sake of, in favour of
my fatherland and the orchestra

And a soprano sings:

enjoying the pleasures of heaven
we have shunned the earth
the tumult of the world
does not reach us in heaven
our lives here are mild and restful

we lead the life of angels
free from troubles, almost living
and all the saints look on

After the war a newspaper writes about the board of the
     Concertgebouw:

> *for years these good dutchmen*
> *followed every order*
> *firing the jewish members*
> *removing mahler and mendelssohn*
> *from the walls*
>
> *one wonders why*
> *so many others*
> *fell in the struggle*
> *or died in camps*

And a soprano sings:

> *deer and hare to roast and eat*
> *run down the public streets*
> *the saints walk past*
> *with nets and bait*
> *the saints are cooks and chefs*

Only the orchestra comes through the war unscathed. The
     fabulous many-headed beast of wood, gut, brass and
     skin – the beast is saved. You hear that in the summer
     of 1945, when it performs Mahler again for the first
     time in years. The chorus sings:

arise, yes,
you will rise
after resting briefly

It is not Mengelberg standing in front of the orchestra, but
in the hall it is impossible to think of anything but his
hand. The boss moves in Mahler.
Oh, how he was lord and master of this music. How, for
fifty years, he moulded the sound like a dictator. He
had created the perfect orchestral machine, so that
what had been built up would be preserved.

arise, yes
you will rise

All thanks to a wave of his hand.
And oh, we were all ear.

The soprano has finished her song and sits down. Next to
her the podium is deserted.
The landscape has gradually become transparent, the sleighs
have disappeared, the sausages have fallen from the
trees. Around us, the petals slowly close.
There was no affirmation, no triumph. There were no
heroes and no jubilation. No one awoke during the
final bars. Mahler wrote an inverted finale.

morendo…

morendo...

The music itself falls asleep. There is just a deep fourth,
    rising and falling in the harps.
When the petals have closed, only a single note can be
    heard, whispering to the depths. A low, repeating
    contra E in the harps.

morendo...

The music itself is stranded. All that is left is an echo of
    paradise.
The audience sits dumbstruck, like before, at a premiere.

And somewhere, in this incomprehensible silence, in
    another place, a Jew is still writing to his love:

one feels so alone
although they are all so kind
and go to such lengths

eternally...

this hanging round abroad
no matter how loving the welcome
one is thwarted on all sides
and finally abandoned

eternally...

And a friend says:

> *art is not politics*
> *if I had done something*
> *I would understand*
> *but I always kept out of everything*

And the Jew whispers:

> *that is Europe's taint*
> *everyone saying*
> *it's none of my business*

Far away is the sound of sleighs.

And heaven... heaven is hung with violins.

ACKNOWLEDGEMENTS

Acknowledgements are made to the editors of the publications below for publishing these poems in translation:

In *The Stinging Fly*, Issue 17 Volume Two, Winter 2010-11
    da capo
    New Year's Greetings
In *Banipal 35 – Writing in Dutch*, Summer 2009
    my aching head
    the subhuman and his habitat
    final chorus
    credo
    What's Left
In *Poetry Review* Vol. 97:3, Autumn 2007
    Turn my Mother
    the subhuman and his habitat
    salve and compresses by candlelight
    the true lover
    wonderful month
In a booklet with the CD, *Dmitri Shostakovich, Op. 147. Susanne van Els (viola), Reinbert de Leeuw (piano)*, October 2007
    winter sonata
In *Revolver* 126, 2005
    final chorus
    credo
    wonderful month
    allegretto from winter sonata
In *Souvenirs exotiques, The Paintings of Tom Liekens*, 2005
    rare dawn

ABOUT RAMSEY NASR

Ramsey Nasr was born in Rotterdam, the Netherlands, in 1974, into a Palestinian-Dutch family. In addition to being a prize-winning author of poetry, essays, dramas, librettos, newspaper articles and opinion pieces, he is a gifted film and theatre actor, having graduated in 1995 from the Antwerp drama school Studio Herman Teirlinck. This year he has returned to acting with a 12-part television drama series to be broadcast in 2011.

In 2009, Ramsey Nasr was voted Poet Laureate of the Netherlands, after having also been a very popular City Poet of Antwerp in 2005. His debut poetry collection, *27 gedichten & Geen lied* (27 Poems & No Song), nominated for the C. Buddingh' Award, 2000, was followed by *onhandig bloesemend* (awkwardly flowering), which won the 2004 Hugues C. Pernath Prize and was reprinted many times, and *onze-lieve-vrouwe-zeppelin* (our lady zeppelin), 2006. These were published together in 2009 as *tussen lelie en waterstofbom: The Early Years* (thousand lilies and hydrogen bomb).

In 2006 Ramsey Nasr was awarded the honorary prize 'Journalist for Peace' by the Humanistisch Vredesberaad (Humanistic Peace Council) and an honorary doctorate from the University of Antwerp. That year he also published *Van de vijand en de muzikant* (Of the enemy and the musician), a collection of his articles on art and politics, including his literary tours to Palestine and the Dutch Antilles.

An inveterate traveller, Ramsey Nasr records his travels in diaries. After a trip to Tanzania with 35 medical students came *Homo safaricus* (2009) and a documentary series *Wildcard:Tanzania*. His journey to Myanmar/Burma with medical students on a humanitarian mission has resulted in a new 5-part television documentary entitled *Wildcard: Myanmar*, and the publication of his latest book *In de gouden buik van Boeddha* (In Buddha's golden belly). Ramsey Nasr is a regular performer of his works in the Netherlands and many other countries, including Georgia, Turkey, Jordan, United Arab Emirates, Indonesia, Palestine, the United Kingdom and the Dutch Antilles, all of these travels contributing enormously to the scope of his works and his outlook on national identity.

More information on his works and activities can be found on his website www.ramseynasr.nl.

ABOUT DAVID COLMER

David Colmer is an Australian author and translator and a long-time resident of Amsterdam. He translates Dutch literature into English in a range of genres and has won several translation awards, most notably the 2009 New South Wales Premier's Translation Prize and PEN Award for his body of work. In 2010 his translation of Gerbrand Bakker's first novel, *The Twin*, won the International IMPAC Dublin Literary Award. He has written a novel and a collection of short stories, both of which have been published in Dutch translation in the Netherlands.

David Colmer first translated Ramsey Nasr's poetry in 2004 for the Rotterdam Poetry International Festival.

ABOUT VICTOR SCHIFERLI

Born in Haarlem, 1967, in the Netherlands, Victor Schiferli is a poet, freelance journalist and editor. He wrote the introduction to *Banipal 35 – Writing in Dutch*. His first poetry collection was published in 2000 and shortlisted for the C. Buddingh' Award. His third, *Toespraak in een struik* (A speech in the bushes), 2008, was shortlisted for the Hugues C. Pernath Prize. He co-edited the literary guidebook *City-Pick: Amsterdam* (Oxygen Books, UK, 2010), and is the poetry reviewer for the daily newspaper *Het Parool*.